Contribitors

L. Ron Hubbard
Jeffrey A. Carver
D. C. Gomez
Candace MacPhie
Jennifer Anne Gordon
Peter Thomas Pontsa
Jonni Jordyn
Fern Brady
John Heldt
Remi Dewitt
Guy Quartley
Davon Ansley
Timothy Jay Smith
Darren Joy
Tim Mulligan
Brian O' Brien
Zwahk Muchoney
Sam Choi
Nicholas Gretener
Andie L. Smith
L. E. Denton

Review Tales
A Book Magazine For Indie Authors

COPYRIGHT   2025
Review Tales Magazine - A Book Magazine for Indie Authors

Founder & Editor in Chief: S. Jeyran Main
Publisher: Review Tales Publishing & Editing Services
Print & Distribution: Ingram Spark
Designs: Pexels
ISBN 978-1-988680-60-6 (Paperback)
ISBN 978-1-988680-61-3 (Digital)
www.jeyranmain.com
For all inquiries, please contact us directly.

Photo Credits from Pexels:
pexels-alpyildizlar-29254561
pexels-rdne-5530743

Editor's Note

Hello Readers,

Welcome to the third issue of Review Tales Book Magazine! I can hardly believe we're already three months in—what a journey it's been!

This magazine thrives because of YOU: the writers, authors, publishers, and readers who make up this incredible community. Your creativity, hard work, and passion for storytelling inspire us every day. Thank you for trusting us to share your words, your art, and your vision with the world. Whether you've featured in these pages, shared our work, or simply taken the time to read and celebrate these stories, we are endlessly grateful for your support.

This issue is packed with talent, and I can't wait for you to dive in! Each feature represents the heart and soul of someone dedicated to their craft—and that's what makes this magazine such a joy to create.

If you're reading this and thinking, "I'd love to be a part of this," then consider this your open invitation! Whether you're an emerging writer, a seasoned author, or a passionate publisher, we'd be thrilled to feature your work. Your story deserves to be shared, and we'd love to help you bring it to life on these pages.

Here's to another month of celebrating the power of words and the vibrant community that makes it all possible. Let's keep the magic alive—one story at a time.

Happy reading,

Jeyran Main

Editor-in-Chief
Review Tales Magazine

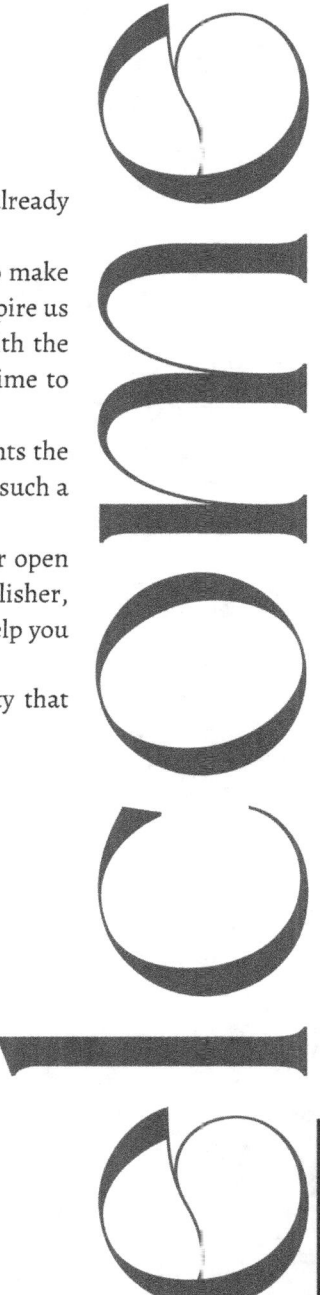

WINTER 2025 | ISSUE 03

BOOK REVIEWS

Review Tales is thrilled to have reached the milestone of over 1,900 book reviews. With this extensive experience, we've had the privilege of exploring a vast range of literature. Our reviews are always impartial and thoughtfully crafted to highlight authors' strengths while inspiring them to keep creating. For this Winter issue, we've handpicked 20 exceptional book reviews to feature.

TO APPLY FOR A BOOK REVIEW VISIT
WWW.JEYRANMAIN.COM

Book Reviews

L. RON HUBBARD PRESENTS WRITERS OF THE FUTURE VOLUME 39: THE BEST NEW SF & FANTASY OF THE YEAR
L. Ron Hubbard

Reviewer: Jeyran Main

L. Ron Hubbard Presents Writers of the Future Volume 39. This is a treasure trove for speculative fiction fans. This annual anthology continues its tradition of spotlighting fresh talent in science fiction and fantasy, delivering an engaging mix of imaginative storytelling, breathtaking artwork, and invaluable writing advice. Edited by industry veterans Dean Wesley Smith and Jody Lynn Nye, the volume features 12 award-winning stories from emerging voices and three bonus tales from established legends Kevin J. Anderson, L. Ron Hubbard, and S. M. Stirling.

The stories span a wide range of themes and styles, ensuring there's something for every reader. Highlights include Devon Bohm's "Kitsune," a poetic and haunting tale of mysterious foxes; David Hankins' "Death and the Taxman," a darkly comedic and inventive twist on the Grim Reaper; and Spencer Sekulin's "The Children of Desolation," an emotionally charged post-apocalyptic journey. The standout feature of these stories is their ability to entertain and provoke thought, showcasing the writers' creativity and potential.

The bonus stories add an extra layer of enjoyment, offering insights into the craft of storytelling from seasoned masters. Kevin J. Anderson's "Fire in the Hole," featuring his beloved character Dan Shamble, Zombie P.I., is a hilarious romp that fans of humorous fantasy will adore. Meanwhile, S. M. Stirling's "Constant Never" presents a perverse and gripping take on classic fantasy tropes, cementing his reputation as a genre master.

Beyond the stories, the anthology includes a 16-page color gallery of stunning artwork and insightful essays on writing and art by contributors like Kristine Kathryn Rusch and Lazarus Chernik. These additions make the collection an invaluable resource for aspiring creators and fans who want to peek behind the curtain of speculative fiction.

This volume exemplifies the enduring appeal of the Writers of the Future series. It's not just a collection of excellent stories—it's a celebration of the genre and a launchpad for the next generation of great storytellers. Whether you're a die-hard fan of science fiction and fantasy or a newcomer curious about the genre, Volume 39 offers a thrilling, thought-provoking, and inspiring experience.

With glowing endorsements from notable authors like Brandon Sanderson and Orson Scott Card and a strong reputation for discovering new talent, L. Ron Hubbard Presents Writers of the Future Volume 39 is a must-read. Dive into this anthology to be amazed, amused, and transported to realms beyond imagination.

THE REEFS OF
TIME
Jeffrey A. Carver

Reviewer: Jeyran Main

Jeffrey A. Carver's The Reefs of Time is an enthralling installment in The Chaos Chronicles, blending breathtaking space opera with intricate time-travel mechanics. As the fifth book in the series, it brings readers back to the thrilling adventures of John Bandicut and his eclectic alien companions as they face a galaxy-threatening challenge.

The novel opens with a tantalizing premise: the Mindaru, an ancient AI menace thought to be destroyed, resurfaces with a new strategy to wreak havoc. Using the star stream—a hyperspatial highway connecting civilizations—the AI hurtles toward humanity's future, threatening annihilation. Carver's depiction of the Starscream is a visual and conceptual marvel, capturing its awe-inspiring beauty and deadly potential.

John Bandicut and his companions are the only ones capable of intervening, but the stakes are higher than ever. The disappearance of key team members forces Bandicut and the resourceful Li-Jared to form a new alliance with Ruall, a pandimensional being, and her goat—a quirky alien whose uniqueness adds humor and heart to the story. Together, they embark on a mission to the planet Karellia, whose unsuspecting inhabitants are at the epicenter of a temporal disturbance with catastrophic implications.

Carver's strength lies in his ability to weave hard science fiction concepts with deeply human (and alien) emotions. The narrative explores themes of sacrifice, camaraderie, and the resilience of life in the face of overwhelming odds. The characters, both old and new, are richly developed, their relationships adding depth to the sweeping galactic stakes.

The world-building is masterful, with Karellia and the star stream vividly brought to life through Carver's descriptive prose. The action sequences are tense and dynamic, while the slower moments delve into existential questions about technology, time, and the consequences of meddling with the past and future.

While The Reefs of Time can stand independently due to Carver's skillful integration of the backstory, readers who follow the series will appreciate the continuity and growth of the characters and overarching plot. The book's pacing is deliberate, allowing for a satisfying buildup to its climactic moments, though some might find the complexity of the science and time-travel mechanics requiring close attention.

In conclusion, The Reefs of Time is a stunning continuation of The Chaos Chronicles, offering a perfect blend of high-stakes adventure, intricate science fiction, and emotional depth. It's a must-read for fans of epic space opera and those who enjoy stories that challenge the boundaries of time and imagination. Prepare to be transported across the galaxy—and through time—in this captivating journey.

DEATH'S INTERN
D. C. Gomez

Reviewer: Jeyran Main

Death's Intern by D.C. Gomez is a wildly entertaining introduction to The Intern Diaries series, an urban fantasy tale brimming with dark humor, quirky characters, and unexpected twists. From the very first page, readers are thrown into the chaotic and hilarious life of Isis Black, a sarcastic musician and waitress who, much to her disbelief, finds herself hired as Death's newest Intern. Utterly untrained in the supernatural, Isis must navigate a bizarre new reality while embarking on a dangerous mission to save her kidnapped best friend, Bob.

The premise is as zany as it sounds: a struggling young woman agreeing to work for Death, dealing with a talking cat, and uncovering mysteries tied to the Horsemen of the Apocalypse. Isis is a refreshing protagonist—relatable, strong-willed, and hilariously cynical. Her dry humor and inner monologues provide plenty of laughs, even as she's faced with daunting supernatural challenges and life-or-death stakes.

One of the book's greatest strengths is its colorful cast of characters. From Constantine, the sarcastic and opinionated talking cat, to Ezekiel, the boy genius, each character adds personality and depth to the story. Their interactions with Isis are comedic and heartfelt, creating a delightful dynamic that keeps the reader engaged. Even Death, typically a figure of fear and finality, is portrayed with charm and humanity.

The plot moves briskly, seamlessly blending action, humor, and moments of genuine emotion. Gomez weaves a clever, unpredictable narrative where supernatural elements and real-world struggles collide. While the story is undeniably lighthearted, it explores deeper themes of loyalty and self-discovery. Isis's journey isn't just about fighting supernatural forces—it's also about finding her place in a much bigger and more dangerous world than she ever imagined.

Another highlight is the world-building in Death's Intern. Gomez introduces readers to a universe where Death is more of a bureaucratic figure than a grim reaper and the supernatural blends effortlessly with the mundane. The Horsemen and other mythological elements enrich the story, offering a fresh take on traditional urban fantasy tropes.

Death's Intern is a must-read if you're a fan of fast-paced, character-driven urban fantasy with plenty of laughs and surprises. With its witty dialogue, memorable characters, and action-packed plot, it's a book that delivers both humor and heart. D.C. Gomez has crafted a unique and thoroughly entertaining story that will leave readers eager for the next installment in the series.

LIFE STRIKES BACK
Candace MacPhie

Reviewer: Jeyran Main

Candace MacPhie's Life Strikes Back, the second installment in the Back in a Year series, takes readers on a raw and emotional journey through the highs and lows of backpacking across Eastern Europe and Turkey in the 1990s. Far from a romanticized travel memoir, MacPhie delivers an honest portrayal of her struggles with grief, culture shock, and the challenges of life on the road while capturing the resilience and growth that come with stepping outside one's comfort zone.

The story picks up with MacPhie and her travel partner, Khadejah, embarking on what was meant to be the trip of a lifetime. The dream of exotic adventures is quickly tempered by harsh realities: relentless rain, disappointing food, unfriendly locals, and the heavy weight of personal grief. Yet, through these challenges, MacPhie's storytelling shines, blending heartfelt introspection with moments of levity as she discovers hidden treasures and unexpected joys in her journey.

A central theme of the book is perseverance in the face of adversity. With the help of her friends, laughter, and the soundtrack of George Michael, MacPhie finds moments of connection and beauty amid the chaos. The vivid descriptions of landscapes, historical sites, and cultural encounters immerse readers in the places she visits, while her candid reflections on mental health and the complexities of solo travel add depth and authenticity.

However, the book doesn't shy away from addressing the darker side of her experiences, including leers, harassment, and an alarming incident that leaves her questioning whether the rewards of travel outweigh the risks. These moments are handled sensitively, emphasizing the emotional toll of such encounters while highlighting MacPhie's courage in sharing her truth.

MacPhie's narrative is as much about self-discovery as it is about travel. Set in the pre-Internet era, the story is infused with a nostalgic charm, capturing the spontaneity and unpredictability of 1990s backpacking. Her witty, unfiltered voice makes for an engaging read, and her ability to balance humor with heavy topics creates an entertaining and profoundly moving memoir.

Life Strikes Back is a compelling and unforgettable read for those who appreciate travel memoirs that go beyond surface-level adventure. It's a story about resilience, friendship, and finding light in the darkest moments. Whether you're a seasoned traveler or an armchair explorer, this book will transport you and leave you reflecting on the transformative power of travel.

PRETTY UGLY
Jennifer Anne Gordon

Reviewer: Jeyran Main

Jennifer Anne Gordon's Pretty/Ugly is a haunting, lyrical dive into a dystopian nightmare that feels eerily close to reality. Combining psychological depth with horror and speculative fiction, Gordon crafts a poignant story about two broken individuals navigating a crumbling world, both externally and internally.

The novel follows Omelia, a social media influencer who masks her grief and emptiness with the fleeting validation of likes and comments, and Sam, a disillusioned politician burdened by familial expectations and his unfulfilled life. Their worlds unravel amid a relentless pandemic and a societal collapse; their stories intersect in profound and unsettling ways. Gordon's portrayal of their struggles is raw and visceral, exposing the fragility of human identity in the face of trauma and existential despair.

Thematically, Pretty/Ugly is more than a horror novel—it's a deep exploration of identity, grief, loneliness, and how we try to mask our pain. Gordon's writing is vivid and hallucinogenic, weaving together a dreamlike narrative that blurs the line between reality and metaphor. Omelia's transformation, symbolized by the sinister black vines creeping across her body, is as much a psychological journey as a physical one. Sam's self-destructive spiral, punctuated by scandal and paranoia, captures the suffocating weight of societal expectations and personal disillusionment.

The dystopian backdrop—a relentless pandemic that may lead to humanity's extinction—is both timely and chilling. Gordon paints this apocalyptic landscape with poetic precision, making it as beautiful as it is terrifying. The narrative is deeply introspective, offering moments of quiet reflection amid the chaos.

Readers who appreciate psychological horror and character-driven stories will find Pretty/Ugly compelling. Comparisons to The Happening and Contagion are apt, but Gordon's novel is her own, blending existential dread with an aching sense of beauty. The book's poignant exploration of early trauma, identity, and societal collapse resonates long after the final page.

While the story leans into its poetic and hallucinogenic style, some readers may find it too abstract or unsettling. However, for those willing to embrace the darkness, Pretty/Ugly offers an unforgettable experience—a meditation on the ephemeral nature of life, the masks we wear, and the fleeting beauty of human connection, even as the world falls apart.

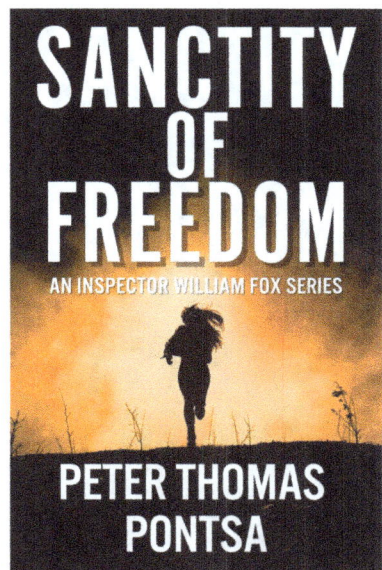

SANCTITY OF FREEDOM
Peter Thomas Pontsa

Reviewer: Jeyran Main

Sanctity of Freedom, the second book in Peter Pontsa's Inspector William Fox series, is a gripping tale that blends personal stakes with international intrigue. The story starts with Inspector William Fox enjoying a peaceful outing with his girlfriend, Tracy Jordan, aboard his cigarette boat, The Midnight Fox. However, their calm is shattered when a police scanner announces that a body is washed ashore. Despite Tracy's objections, Fox is compelled to investigate.

On-site, the Montreal police discover a note on the victim addressed to Fox's close friend and taekwondo master, Mr. Kim. The note hints at a connection to Kim's long-lost sister, Mi-Cha, who was kidnapped as a child and taken to North Korea. Believing she may still be alive, Kim seeks Fox's help to uncover the truth and bring her home.

The plot thickens when Fox and FBI Special Agent Patrick Reilly are drawn into the brutal assassination of a Canadian diplomat and two Australian intelligence operatives. As their investigation unfolds, Kim pursues leads about his sister that point to the shadowy operatives of North Korea's Bureau 39—a secretive organization infamous for its illicit activities to fund the regime.

What follows is a dangerous and high-stakes journey that intertwines Fox's pursuit of justice with Kim's quest for his sister. The narrative takes readers through geopolitical intrigue, betrayal, and moral dilemmas. From the diplomatic circles of Canada to the perilous streets of Pyongyang, the story propels its characters into a deadly game of cat and mouse.

Pontsa masterfully balances two compelling threads: Fox's hunt for a cunning assassin and Kim's profoundly personal mission to confront the man responsible for taking his sister. The novel explores themes of loyalty, sacrifice, and the lengths one will go to protect their loved ones. The partnership between Fox and Kim provides a poignant emotional core, while the inclusion of FBI agent Reilly adds an extra layer of dynamic tension and international cooperation.

With its intricate plot, richly developed characters, and action-packed sequences, Sanctity of Freedom delivers a thrilling ride. Fans of crime dramas and political thrillers will appreciate the novel's blend of personal and geopolitical stakes. This story challenges its protagonists to confront their pasts and the shadowy forces threatening their futures.

THE LOST ART OF MAGIC
Jonni Jordyn

Reviewer: Jeyran Main

Jonni Jordyn's The Lost Art of Magic: Tome I is an enchanting start to a riveting fantasy series, weaving together elements of mysticism, danger, and self-discovery. Set against the hauntingly atmospheric bayou backdrop, this first installment introduces readers to Destiny, a sixteen-year-old girl whose rediscovery of long-forgotten magic sets her on a collision course with danger.

Destiny's lineage of psychic women has always set her apart, but her accidental awakening of ancient magic draws the attention of dangerous figures from old clans. These adversaries, determined to claim the power for themselves, see Destiny as a threat that must be eliminated. Jordyn's narrative deftly explores themes of heritage, the weight of responsibility, and the clash between innocence and ambition.

The richly drawn bayou setting is more than just a backdrop; it's a character in its own right. Jordyn brings the environment to life with vivid descriptions of its murky waters, lush vegetation, and eerie stillness, adding a layer of foreboding that complements the story's darker elements. The magic itself is intricately detailed, blending ancient traditions with a fresh, modern twist that makes the rediscovery of this lost art feel both wondrous and authentic.

Destiny is a relatable and compelling protagonist, grappling with her newfound powers and the immense responsibility they bring. Her journey from an ordinary teenager to a young woman navigating a perilous world of magic and betrayal is captivating and emotionally resonant. Jordyn skillfully balances her moments of vulnerability with flashes of courage and determination, making her a character readers will root for.

The supporting cast adds depth and complexity to the story, with both allies and enemies shrouded in mystery and intrigue. The antagonists—descendants of the old clans willing to do whatever it takes to claim the magic for themselves—are chillingly ruthless, adding a palpable sense of danger to every page.

What sets The Lost Art of Magic: Tome I apart is its seamless blend of action, suspense, and introspection. The stakes are high, the pacing relentless, and the twists unexpected, keeping readers on edge as they follow Destiny's perilous journey. The story also hints at deeper secrets and rich lore that promises to be further explored in the subsequent books of the series.

Jonni Jordyn has crafted a spellbinding tale that will appeal to fans of young adult fantasy and readers who love stories of ancient magic, powerful heroines, and the fight against overwhelming odds. With its captivating world-building, strong character development, and thrilling narrative, The Lost Art of Magic: Tome I is an unforgettable beginning to what promises to be an extraordinary series.

UNITED VIDDEN
Fern Brady

Reviewer: Jeyran Main

United Vidden by Fern Brady is an exhilarating and highly creative work of Science Fantasy that immerses readers in a universe where royal drama, interplanetary politics, and complex characters create a genuinely engaging experience. The novel introduces Princess Verena, the rightful heir to the throne of Dravidia on the planet Jorn, who, after being denied her birthright by her father, makes the critical mistake of running away. Her departure, timed just before her arranged wedding to the heir of the Principality of Aulden, sets off a chain of events that spirals into war. When Verena eventually returns to her home planet in a desperate attempt to reclaim her throne, she finds it has already been conquered by Prince Amiel ra Aulden, the man she was supposed to marry.

The novel explores Verena's journey to regain her birthright and win back the trust of her people. Her character's growth is captivating as she faces difficult decisions and comes to terms with the consequences of her actions. Amiel, the charming but enigmatic prince, is equally compelling. His motivations are complex, and as the story unfolds, the lines between ally and enemy blur, creating an intriguing dynamic that keeps the reader on edge.

The story's backdrop is just as captivating as its characters. Brady skillfully blends elements of royal court intrigue, reminiscent of Elizabethan times, with sweeping space opera adventure. The political landscape of the Vidden continent and its complex relationships with other planets in the galaxy add layers of depth to the narrative. The involvement of magical religious sects like Rajin, Nijar, and the Elamin Order further enriches the plot, infusing it with an additional sense of mysticism and power struggles beyond mere earthly concerns.

United Vidden's blend of action and human emotion sets it apart from other space operas. Brady's writing style pulls the reader into a world where stakes are high, and every decision carries immense weight. The novel's unpredictability keeps the reader thoroughly engaged, and just when you think you know where the story is headed, Brady throws in a twist you never saw coming.

United Vidden is an exceptional blend of space opera, royal intrigue, and magical politics. It leaves readers eager to know what will happen next. With its unforgettable characters, dynamic plot, and richly detailed world, this novel is a promising introduction to a series with limitless potential. If you're a fan of both science fiction and fantasy, United Vidden is sure to captivate you.

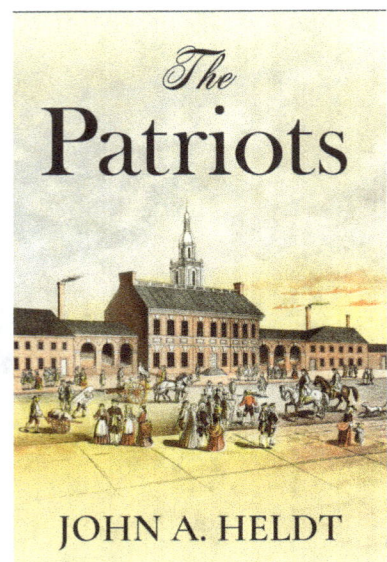

THE PATRIOTS
JOHN A. HELDT

Reviewer: Jeyran Main

The Patriots by John A. Heldt is a captivating time-travel adventure that blends history, humor, romance, and emotional growth. As the first book in the Stone Shed series, it sets the stage for a remarkable journey through time while establishing strong, relatable characters and a compelling, multi-layered narrative.

The story follows 22-year-old Noah Maclean, a young man returning home to an emotional scene: his beloved grandfather is dying, and a hidden letter reveals a long-buried family secret. To Noah's astonishment, he discovers that he is the keeper of a mysterious stone shed, an enigmatic structure capable of sending people through time. Along with his mischievous and curious younger brother, 15-year-old Jake, Noah embarks on an adventure they will never forget.

Their journey takes them back to 1776, to the heart of Philadelphia, during one of the most pivotal moments in American history. This is a time of revolution, where the founding fathers are crafting the Declaration of Independence and shaping the destiny of a fledgling nation. What begins as a thrilling historical field trip to the past quickly transforms into a deeply personal and transformative experience.

As the brothers navigate this world, they form bonds with two spirited young women—the daughters of a local furniture maker. These relationships add a romantic and emotional depth to their adventure, grounding the fantastical elements with heartfelt human connections. At the same time, Noah and Jake grapple with their knowledge of future events and the weight of their inherited powers.

Heldt's storytelling perfectly blends humor, tension, and poignant moments. Readers will find themselves laughing at the brothers' witty exchanges and feeling their heartbreak as they adjust to the challenges of a completely unfamiliar world. The emotional complexity of their journey, particularly the unbreakable bond between the two brothers, is both touching and profound.

Though the main storyline concludes satisfactorily, many intriguing plot threads are left open, leaving readers eagerly anticipating the next installment in this promising trilogy. The Patriots deliver a rich historical context, vivid characters, and a perfect blend of adventure and heart. Fans of time-travel fiction with a historical twist will find this book utterly absorbing and eagerly await the continuation of Noah and Jake's journey.

SOMEWHAT LOST
Remi Dewitt

Reviewer: Jeyran Main

Somewhat Lost: It Was One Bottle of Wine by Remi DeWitt is a fun, lighthearted sci-fi adventure that takes readers on a quirky, entertaining journey through the cosmos. The story begins with Debbie waking up in the clutches of alien captors, only to be saved by a mysterious woman with no memory of her identity. This leads to a whirlwind escape from the aliens and an unexpected partnership between Debbie and her rescuer, whom Debbie names Ellen due to her knack for kicking alien butt.

As the pair travel across the universe, they search for answers about Ellen's past, the aliens' motives, and the mysterious nature of their situation. The humor in this tale is absurd and endearing, with Debbie's dry wit and the oddball circumstances they encounter along the way keeping the tone light and enjoyable. The premise of a sci-fi story built around first contact and alien abductions is familiar.

The dynamic between Debbie and Ellen is a key highlight as their bond grows stronger throughout the adventure. The mystery surrounding Ellen's identity and the aliens' intentions adds a layer of intrigue, but the humor and the oddities of the universe truly shine in this novel. DeWitt skillfully balances moments of action with comedic exchanges, keeping the pacing fast and the story lighthearted.

While the book focuses heavily on its comedic elements, it doesn't shy away from exploring themes of identity, friendship, and self-discovery. Ellen's journey to uncover her past mirrors Debbie's growth as she learns to embrace the bizarre and unpredictable nature of the universe. The contrast between the characters—Ellen's mysterious, no-nonsense demeanor and Debbie's sarcastic, everywoman perspective—creates a compelling dynamic that keeps readers engaged.

Somewhat Lost: It Was One Bottle of Wine is a charming and offbeat take on the sci-fi genre. While it doesn't take itself too seriously, it's an enjoyable romp through space filled with quirky characters, humorous situations, and an engaging plot. This book is delightful for fans of lighthearted, first-contact stories with a healthy dose of humor. It's a refreshing reminder that even in the vastness of the universe, laughter and connection can help us navigate the unknown.

LIVING
Davon Ansley

Reviewer: Jeyran Main

Living... by Davon Ansley is an evocative and heartfelt poetry collection that delves deep into the intricacies of modern life. Set for release on June 27, 2024, this compilation of 100 poems invites readers to explore the mundane and profound, offering a vivid portrait of contemporary existence.

The poems seamlessly weave through various themes, inviting readers to reflect on their journeys, memories, and aspirations. Whether exploring the simplicity of everyday moments or unraveling the complexities of life's challenges, these verses are crafted to inspire and resonate on a profoundly personal level. Each poem serves as a window into the human condition, capturing emotions and experiences that are both universal and intimate.

What sets Living... apart is its thoughtful organization. Divided into ten thematic sections, each containing ten poems, the collection provides a cohesive structure that guides readers through exploring topics like loyalty, resilience, love, and self-discovery. This approach allows for a dynamic reading experience, where each section builds on the last, creating a sense of progression and connection.

The beauty of this collection lies in its honesty and accessibility. Ansley's writing is refreshingly candid, free from pretense or hidden agendas. Instead, it offers open, unfiltered reflections that speak directly to the heart. Readers seeking insight, comfort, or simply a moment of connection will find solace within these pages. The poet's ability to articulate the human experience with clarity and sensitivity ensures that every reader will find something to relate to and cherish.

Beyond its emotional depth, Living... is a celebration of the artistry of words. Ansley's skillful use of language brings each poem to life, drawing readers into vivid imagery and poignant moments. The collection reminds readers of the power of poetry to illuminate life's complexities while providing comfort and inspiration.

Whether you're a lifelong poetry lover or a genre newcomer, Living... offers an engaging and rewarding experience. It's a book to return to repeatedly, finding new layers of meaning with each reading. Dive into this remarkable collection and let its words guide you on a journey of reflection, self-discovery, and appreciation for the beauty of life's intricacies.

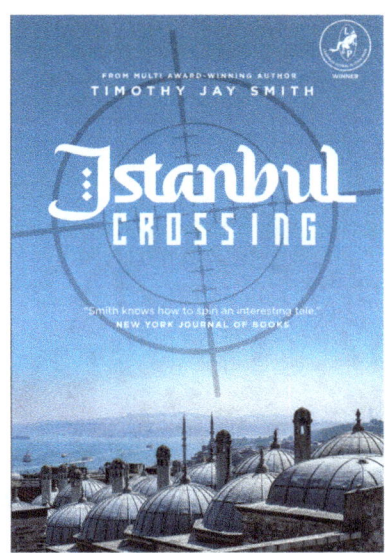

ISTANBUL CROSSING
Timothy Jay Smith

Reviewer: Jeyran Main

Istanbul Crossing by Timothy Jay Smith is a gripping literary thriller that pulls readers into the harrowing world of Ahdaf, a Syrian refugee and people smuggler entangled in a web of danger, secrecy, and impossible choices. The novel intricately explores themes of survival, identity, and love as Ahdaf faces threats from both ISIS and the CIA while also grappling with the burden of hiding his sexuality in a world where such an identity is life-threatening.

Ahdaf's existence is defined by peril. As a smuggler, he helps others escape the ravages of war-torn Syria, but the risk lies in the secret he keeps hidden from those around him: his love for another man. In a society ruled by ISIS, where homosexuality is punishable by death, Ahdaf's sexual identity could cost him his life. The tension ratchets up as Ahdaf becomes embroiled in a high-stakes game, working as a double agent, smuggling individuals for both ISIS and the CIA. His moral compass is tested when he falls for one of his clients, forcing him to confront the harrowing consequences of his choices.

Smith's writing is evocative, drawing readers into the complex landscape of Istanbul, where cultures and conflicts collide in a volatile environment. The novel skillfully intertwines political intrigue with personal stakes as Ahdaf's journey becomes about more than mere survival—confronting his deepest fears, desires, and identity. The emotional tension between Ahdaf and the characters he meets is palpable, especially as he navigates the blurred lines between love, duty, and betrayal in a world where trust is fleeting and survival is everything.

The novel explores the refugee experience, offering a nuanced, human perspective on a crisis often reduced to headlines. Smith doesn't just highlight the physical dangers faced by refugees; he also delves into the psychological and emotional toll of living in constant fear. Ahdaf's internal struggles—balancing loyalty to his family, his survival, and his burgeoning feelings for another man—drive the plot, keeping readers on edge throughout.

Istanbul Crossing is a remarkable thriller that combines political intrigue with profound emotional depth. Smith delivers a haunting, moving narrative that reflects the resilience of the human spirit in the face of insurmountable odds. For fans of literary thrillers, political drama, and stories of survival, this novel is an absolute must-read.

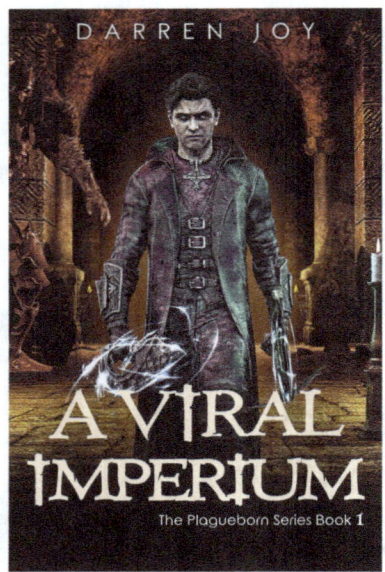

A VIRAL IMPERIUM
Darren Joy

Reviewer: Jeyran Main

Darren Joy's A Viral Imperium is the first installment in The Plagueborn Series, a dark epic fantasy that expertly blends humor, magic, and apocalyptic stakes. With a richly developed world and a gripping narrative, this novel is essential for fans of darker, more intricate fantasy tales that challenge the mind and the heart.

The story takes place in a fragile world that has only begun to heal from the ravages of plagues and purges that nearly destroyed it. Yet, peace proves fleeting, and chaos again looms on the horizon. The story follows Threadfin Todder, a morally complex protagonist who embarks on a desperate journey to save his sister while being relentlessly pursued by a shapeshifter who will stop at nothing to capture him. Along the way, he faces external enemies and the dark magic threatening to consume him. This struggle offers readers a layered, intense character arc that keeps them invested in his fate from beginning to end.

Meanwhile, Princess Aiyana Todralan is embroiled in her fight for survival as a murderous usurper seizes the throne. Her path converges with Threadfin's in unexpected and thrilling ways, creating a dual narrative that drives the tension and suspense throughout the book. Both characters ultimately confront themselves with the revelation of an ancient, overwhelming force that threatens to undo existence. The stakes rise exponentially as the threat looms, bringing the plot to exhilarating heights.

One of the standout features of A Viral Imperium is Joy's intricate world-building. The imperium feels alive, populated with strange creatures, deep power dynamics, and mythological underpinnings, making the setting rich and immersive. The dark magic that permeates the world is terrifying and fascinating, adding depth and mystery to the narrative. Joy also skillfully weaves moments of dark humor throughout, providing a much-needed counterbalance to the book's intense themes and making it both thrilling and darkly entertaining.

What truly sets A Viral Imperium apart is its seamless fusion of epic battles, metaphysical elements, and character-driven storytelling. This thrilling blend of action, philosophy, and emotional depth will captivate fans of works like Mark Lawrence's The Broken Empire and Glen Cook's The Black Company.

With its gripping plot, richly developed characters, and imaginative world, A Viral Imperium is a strong start to what promises to be an unforgettable series. It's a dark, thrilling tale that leaves readers eagerly awaiting the next chapter in The Plagueborn Series.

SNITCHLAND: THE GRAPHIC NOVEL
Tim Mulligan

Reviewer: Jeyran Main

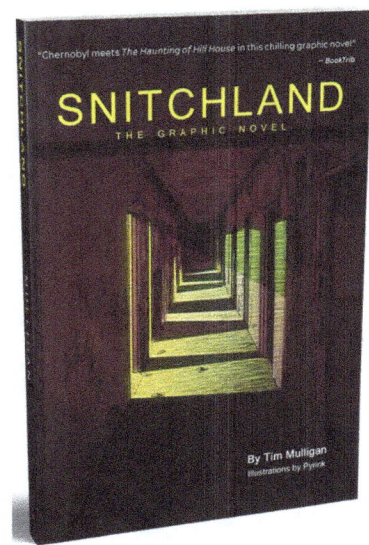

Snitchland: The Graphic Novel by Tim Mulligan is a gripping and suspenseful continuation of the Witchland series. It blends political intrigue, family drama, and the supernatural into a haunting tale that simultaneously captivates and disturbs. Following the success of Witchland, Mulligan delivers a chilling sequel that takes readers deeper into the dark, toxic world surrounding an apparent nuclear accident in one of the most contaminated places in the Western Hemisphere.

The story centers on a family recently relocated from Seattle, who find themselves grappling with the sudden and tragic death of one of the fathers in the accident. The family members struggle with both their grief and the overwhelming uncertainty of the circumstances surrounding the death. During the funeral, a mysterious co-worker of the deceased reveals that she had previously raised concerns about the cause of the accident to management. This sets off a chain of events that spirals into family trauma, political machinations, and an eerie descent into the occult. Mulligan masterfully intertwines the personal and the supernatural, transforming Snitchland into more than just a ghost story—it becomes a powerful meditation on grief, secrecy, and the unforeseen consequences of uncovering uncomfortable truths.

Illustrator Pyrink's stunning artwork is one of the highlights of the graphic novel. The visuals enhance the eerie atmosphere of the story, visually representing the creeping sense of dread that permeates the narrative. Pyrink's art doesn't just complement the writing. Still, it amplifies it, creating an experience where the unsettling imagery brings the story to life in ways that would be impossible in traditional prose. The artwork conveys the emotional depth of the character's struggles and the mounting tension in the world that Mulligan has created. Mulligan's writing and Pyrink's visuals work perfectly, giving the story a dark, foreboding tone that never lets up.

Despite the weighty themes of the graphic novel, Snitchland also manages to infuse moments of dark humor, adding complexity to its narrative. These lighter moments deepen the story's emotional impact, making it more than a straightforward horror tale. The characters, particularly the grieving husband and the mysterious co-worker, are well-developed, and their evolving relationships lend emotional gravity to the supernatural elements. Their journey through trauma and secrets makes the final revelations all the more profound.

A brilliant sequel to Witchland, Snitchland is a must-read for fans of graphic novels that expertly blend horror with thought-provoking commentary on society, personal loss, and the cost of uncovering the truth. With its combination of atmospheric artwork, complex characters, and eerie plot, this graphic novel will leave readers thinking long after the final page.

THE ADVENTURES OF KOZMOS LOVEJOY
Patrick O'Brien

Reviewer: Jeyran Main

Patrick O'Brien, writing as Brian Ahern, delivers a transformative and deeply personal tale in The Adventures of Kozmos Lovejoy. Set against the countercultural backdrop of the late 1960s, this memoir-philosophy hybrid offers readers an evocative journey of self-discovery, spiritual exploration, and universal connection. Blending mysticism, psychedelics, and personal awakening, the story captures the spirit of an era of exploration and transformation.

Kozmos Lovejoy, the young artist at the center of the story, embodies the essence of the time. His fascination with psychedelics, Jungian therapy, and spiritual mythology sets the stage for a vivid adventure that blurs the boundaries between dreams and reality. From his surreal vision of a Renaissance banquet to his encounter with the girl from his dreams in the jungles of Puerto Vallarta, Mexico, Kozmos's journey is as much about the mystical as it is about the physical. The narrative constantly challenges the reader's perception of reality, inviting them to explore a world where the boundaries of the conscious and subconscious are in flux.

The narrative unfolds with rich descriptions of Kozmo's travels, from the lush jungles of Mexico to the deserts of the American Southwest and the peaks of the French Alps. Along the way, Kozmos uncovers ancient wisdom, participates in the symbolic Feast of Knowledge, and learns the secrets of stardust—a revelation that speaks to the collective awakening of global consciousness. These experiences lead Kozmos on a path of personal growth and point to a larger, more interconnected world.

O'Brien's writing is lyrical and thought-provoking, weaving personal experiences with profound philosophical insights. The book's themes of divine potential, self-awareness, and surrendering to the unknown resonate deeply, inspiring readers to reflect on their journeys. Including Jungian concepts and spiritual teachings adds intellectual depth, making the story a multi-layered exploration of human consciousness.

While the book tackles complex ideas, it remains engaging thanks to O'Brien's storytelling prowess. His ability to capture the wonder, struggle, and transformation of Kozmo's journey makes the narrative as emotionally resonant as it is intellectually stimulating. O'Brien's vivid descriptions and keen insight into the human condition immerse the reader.

The Adventures of Kozmos Lovejoy celebrates life's mysteries and the courage to embrace them. It's an inspiring read for anyone seeking meaning, connection, and a glimpse into the divine potential within us all. Perfect for fans of philosophical memoirs and spiritual adventures, this book is a gem that leaves a lasting impression.

Heaven's Kin

Zwahk Muchoney

Heaven's Kin by Zwahk Muchoney is the second installment in the series, released on June 7, 2024. This short story collection delves into the celestial siblings' lives and struggles, primarily focusing on the angelic family dynamics in Heaven. The novel presents a fascinating, fictionalized exploration of the complex relationships among the brothers and sisters of Heaven, framed by an ever-present threat: Lucifer, the mad angel.

The stories within Heaven's Kin take readers on diverse, thought-provoking journeys. From Satan and Michael sharing drinks in Mexico to Jophiel aiding a beautiful wastrel in finding love to Raphael grappling with a plague in Heaven, each tale explores the various challenges the angels face as they navigate their celestial existence. The characters' journeys are filled with deep personal struggles, divine intervention, and philosophical questions about pride, loyalty, and redemption.

At the core of Heaven's Kin is the story of Lucifer, the first-born angel who once embodied beauty and light. As the eldest of the celestial siblings, he was deeply admired and loved, and his influence was immense. However, Lucifer's pride grew overwhelmingly, leading to a catastrophic decision that caused a civil war among the angels. The rebellion against God and the resulting fall from grace turned Lucifer from a beloved figure into the embodiment of darkness and despair.

The book draws inspiration from biblical themes, particularly from the passage in Isaiah 14:14, where Lucifer declares, "I will ascend higher than the highest clouds; I will be the Most High." This moment of defiance marks a pivotal shift in the story, setting the stage for Lucifer's fall and the creation of the fallen angels who would forever walk the Earth as devils. The narrative captures this rebellion's emotional and spiritual fallout, offering readers a glimpse into the consequences of pride and disobedience.

Through these interconnected stories, Heaven's Kin highlights themes of divine creation, cosmic battles, and the ongoing struggle between good and evil. The book's emotional complexity and philosophical depth make it a thought-provoking read for those who enjoy celestial mythology and stories of divine conflict. With its compelling characters and epic scope, Heaven's Kin is a captivating addition to the series.

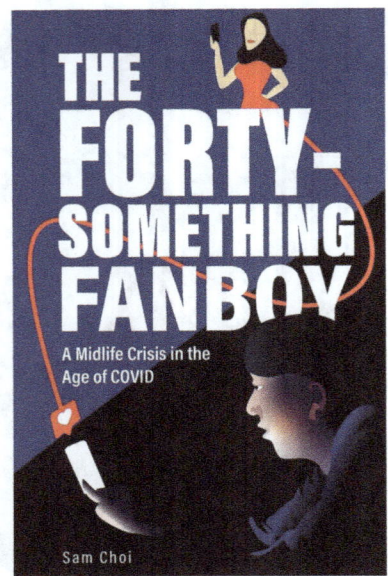

THE FORTY–SOMETHING FANBOY: A MIDLIFE CRISIS IN THE AGE OF COVID
Sam Choi

Reviewer: Jeyran Main

The Forty-Something Fanboy: A Midlife Crisis in the Age of COVID by Sam Choi is a poignant and thought-provoking exploration of identity, loneliness, and self-discovery. The novel centers around David Yi, a recently divorced, middle-aged Korean American man who finds himself at a crossroads in life. Struggling with personal and professional challenges, his isolation deepens during the COVID-19 pandemic, making his already fractured existence more intense and palpable. David's journey through this crisis becomes both comedic and deeply moving as he grapples with issues of cultural identity, familial bonds, and personal growth.

David lives a quiet, disconnected life in a sparse one-bedroom apartment, distanced from his friends and from a new romantic relationship with Yoon-Mi, with whom he has difficulty connecting. His internal struggles with intimacy, aging parents, and the pressures of his job pile up as he finds himself spiraling. Seeking an escape, David's attention turns to a young Korean social media influencer, leading to an obsession that is as exhilarating as embarrassing. This obsession, at first a fleeting distraction, forces David to confront his insecurities, revealing the depth of his internal crisis.

As his emotional unraveling continues, David travels to Korea—a decision that seems rash initially but becomes a transformative moment in his life. David uncovers long-buried family secrets in Korea, including his grandfather's mysterious disappearance and his father's hidden past. These revelations force him to confront his heritage and his family's history. Through this process, David begins to heal, reconciling with his family and identity. His journey culminates in a symbolic act of reconnecting with his heritage: giving his daughter a Korean name. This act signifies David's attempt to reclaim his previously suppressed cultural roots.

Choi's narrative expertly balances humor and tragedy, making David's story relatable and deeply human. His exploration of Korean, Korean American, and broader American values offers insightful commentary on the complexities of cultural identity. The novel beautifully captures the universal experience of navigating midlife crisis, love, and self-realization. Through David's journey, Choi invites readers to reflect on their struggles with identity, loneliness, and the pursuit of meaning.

The Forty-Something Fanboy is a powerful, emotional journey of self-discovery. With its blend of humor, cultural insight, and heartfelt moments, it is an unforgettable read for anyone grappling with their moments of crisis or seeking to understand the complexities of cultural identity.

BENDING THE ARC
Nicholas Gretener

Reviewer: Jeyran Main

Bending the Arc by Nicholas Gretener is a fast-paced legal thriller that dives deep into the intricacies of justice, corporate power, and the legal system. This first entry in the LawForce series introduces readers to Jonathan Hendrix, the youngest U.S. Attorney General in history, determined to reshape the legal landscape. Hendrix's mission is to curb the runaway civil jury awards destabilizing the economy, and he recruits Steve Shane, a brilliant and ambitious commercial litigator, to help him in this cause.

Shane, a young attorney who rejected the conventional path of big law firms, has built his reputation as a respected commercial litigator. However, Hendrix needs him for something more: creating a government-supported legal SWAT team called LawForce, designed to intervene in high-stakes cases where one side is at a clear disadvantage. The team's first assignment takes them into the high-stakes world of environmental litigation, pitting them against the formidable Green Action Coalition (GAC), an influential activist group, in a case involving Wildcat Oil & Gas.

Wildcat, a mid-sized oil and gas company, faces a series of environmental accidents that, according to GAC, are not random but indicative of negligence. The ecological group demands astronomical damages, threatening to obliterate Wildcat in a single blow. Conversely, GAC is represented by a prestigious law firm, Todd Ives Tillington, with the formidable Andrew Tillington III at the helm. Wildcat appears hopelessly outclassed—until Shane and the LawForce team step in to level the playing field.

As Shane and his team dig deeper into the case, they quickly realize there's much more at play than just a legal battle. The twists and turns in the case lead them through a maze of corporate intrigue, legal maneuvering, and unexpected alliances. The stakes are high, and the explosive courtroom finale promises to be thrilling and thought-provoking.

Gretener's writing is sharp, making complex legal strategies accessible without sacrificing depth. The characters, particularly Shane, are compelling and well-developed, and the fast-paced plot keeps the tension high throughout. The novel's exploration of justice, corporate power, and legal ethics offers plenty of food for thought, while its gripping narrative ensures readers remain engaged until the end.

Bending the Arc is a must-read for fans of legal thrillers and corporate intrigue. With a well-crafted plot, rich character development, and timely themes, Gretener has delivered a strong start to what promises to be a captivating series.

COVALENCE
Andie L. Smith

Reviewer: Jeyran Main

In Covalence, Andie L. Smith's debut novel, readers are thrust into a dystopian world where tradition, societal expectations, and personal freedom collide. Seventeen-year-old Mineral Vyotto is determined to escape the oppressive City and its ritualistic Covalence Ceremony, a practice that forces individuals to bond with another of their Kind. To avoid the Ceremony she sees as a trap, Mineral secretly builds a plane in a hidden cavern, dreaming of freedom beyond the City gates.

However, when the Covalence Ceremony is unexpectedly moved up, Mineral is nearly caught by the City's authorities. Her escape plans take a sudden and complicated turn when she finds herself entangled with Amory Thames, an arrogant and opinionated Orderly with influential parents who could destroy her chance at freedom. Despite their differences, Mineral and Amory must reluctantly work together to uncover a way to escape the City before the Ceremony forces their lives to follow a predetermined path.

Tension builds as Mineral and Amory race against time, with only four weeks left to find a way out before the Ceremony. Throughout their journey, the duo faces physical danger and the challenge of keeping Society's darkest secret hidden—one that could have catastrophic consequences for everyone they love. The narrative expertly intertwines themes of rebellion, survival, and the search for freedom, with Mineral's internal struggles serving as a powerful reflection of the more significant societal issues at play.

The author's world-building is immersive and thought-provoking, presenting a society where the value of individuality and personal choice is weighed against the rigidity of tradition. The chemistry between Mineral and Amory adds a dynamic layer to the plot, transforming the story from a fight for freedom into a profoundly personal exploration of trust, compromise, and sacrifice.

Covalence is a thrilling ride, filled with unexpected twists and emotional stakes that keep readers on the edge of their seats. As Mineral and Amory face mounting pressure, they learn that escaping the City may not be as simple as outrunning the Ceremony but rather as understanding the forces that have shaped their lives—and deciding whether or not they can break free from them. A must-read for dystopian fiction fans, Covalence offers heart-pounding action and a powerful message about the cost of freedom.

CROSSING THE BLUE RIDGE: A TALE OF KING'S MOUNTAIN
L. E. Denton

Reviewer: Jeyran Main

L. E. Denton's Crossing the Blue Ridge: A Tale of King's Mountain is a compelling historical novel that transports readers to the turbulent years of the American Revolution. Set in 1774, the story follows Caleb Anders, a young man desperate to escape an oppressive home life, and his friend Nate Daniels as they embark on a dangerous journey across the rugged frontier. Their adventure is a quest for personal freedom and a confrontation with the growing unrest that would lead to the Revolution.

The novel beautifully captures the spirit of the time, focusing on Caleb and Nate as they navigate not only the harsh wilderness of Virginia and the Blue Ridge Mountains but also the moral dilemma they face—whether to remain and defend their community from the Cherokee or join the fight for independence under General George Washington. Their journey is deeply personal, shaped by their evolving friendship and the weight of the revolutionary decisions ahead.

Denton's immersive writing style brings the landscapes and hardships of frontier life to life. The descriptions of the wilderness are vivid and atmospheric, allowing readers to feel the challenges of survival and the mounting pressure of war. Equally important is exploring the bond between Caleb and Nate, with their friendship growing and changing as they face trials and make life-altering decisions. The emotional depth of their relationship adds a layer of complexity to the plot, making it more than just a historical narrative but a story of personal growth and loyalty.

A standout aspect of the novel is Denton's focus on the Battle of King's Mountain, a pivotal yet often overlooked event in the Revolutionary War. By entering the story around this moment, Denton sheds light on the unsung heroes who fought in this battle, highlighting their bravery and determination in the face of overwhelming odds. This focus on lesser-known figures provides a fresh perspective on the American Revolution, making the story feel both historically significant and deeply human.

Crossing the Blue Ridge is a stirring and inspirational tale of courage, friendship, and the pursuit of freedom. Through Caleb and Nate's journey, Denton offers a rich, detailed account of a critical moment in American history. This novel is a must-read for fans of Revolutionary War fiction, providing a captivating and thought-provoking experience that will resonate with readers long after the final page.

www.ingramcontent.com/pod-product-compliance
Lightning Source LLC
Chambersburg PA
CBHW081542120626
46550CB00009B/2837